Earth-Friendly Clay Crafts in 5 Easy Steps

Anna Llimós

Enslow Elementary

an imprint of

Enslow Publishers, Inc.

40 Industrial Road
Box 398
Berkeley Heights, NJ 07922
USA

http://www.enslow.com

Note to Kids and Parents: Getting earth-friendly materials is easy to do. Just look around your house for containers, wrappers, and other things you would throw out. Some of these recyclable materials may include plastic, paper, cardboard, cork, and cloth. The materials used in this book are suggestions. If you do not have an item, use something similar. Use any color material and paint that you wish. Use your imagination!

Safety Note: Be sure to ask for help from an adult, if needed, to complete these crafts.

Enslow Elementary, an imprint of Enslow Publishers, Inc.

Enslow Elementary® is a registered trademark of Enslow Publishers, Inc.

Translated from the Spanish edition by Stacey Juana Pontoriero.
Edited and produced by Enslow Publishers, Inc.

Library of Congress Cataloging-in-Publication Data
Llimós Plomer, Anna.
  [Plastilina (2005). English]
  Earth-friendly clay crafts in 5 easy steps / Anna Llimós.
      pages cm — (Earth-friendly crafts in 5 easy steps)
  Translation of: Plastilina / Anna Llimós. — Barcelona : Parramón Paidotribo, 2005.
  Translated from the Spanish edition by Stacey Juana Pontoriero.
  Includes bibliographical references and index.
  Summary: "Provides step-by-step instructions on how to create fourteen simple clay crafts and includes a vegan recipe for homemade clay" —Provided by publisher.
  ISBN 978-0-7660-4189-9
  1. Modeling—Juvenile literature. I. Title.
  TT916.L5913 2012
  731.4'2—dc23
                        2012013432
Future edition:
Paperback ISBN 978-1-4644-0309-5

Originally published in Spanish under the title *Plastilina.*
Copyright © 2005 Parramón Paidotribo-World Rights
Published by Parramón Paidotribo, S.L., Badalona, Spain

Production: Sagrafic, S.L.
Text: Anna Llimós
Illustrator: Nos & Soto

Printed in Spain
112012 Indice, S.L., Barcelona, Spain
10 9 8 7 6 5 4 3 2 1

To Our Readers: We have done our best to make sure all Internet addresses in this book were active and appropriate when we went to press. However, the author and the publishers have no control over and assume no liability for the material available on those Internet sites or on other Web sites they may link to. Any comments or suggestions can be sent by e-mail to comments@enslow.com or to the address on the back cover.

Contents

**You may want to try this vegan clay recipe to make the crafts in this book.

Vegan Clay Recipe

2 cups of flour
1 cup of salt
1 1/2 tablespoons of vegetable oil
1 tablespoon of corn starch mixed in 2 tablespoons of cold water
2 cups of hot water
food coloring

1. Mix everything in a saucepan and cook at low heat, stirring until the dough is thick and dry, about five minutes.
2. Let the dough cool and divide it into pieces.
3. Make a deep indent into each piece and add food coloring.
4. Knead the dough until the color is even.
5. The clay will dry in about a day or two. Store the unused clay in an airtight container for next time.

**Ask an adult to help you!

Stick Puppet

1 Model the head. Add eyes, a nose, and a mouth. Stick the head onto a dowel.

MATERIALS

air-drying clay–different colors
1 wooden dowel
rolling pin
plastic knife

2 Roll out four long, thin pieces of clay. Wrap two of them around the dowel to make the body. Wrap the other two pieces around the head for the hat.

3 Use a rolling pin to flatten out a piece of clay. Decorate it as you wish.

4 Use a plastic knife to cut out a rectangle from the sheet of clay. Wrap it around the puppet to make a skirt.

5 Roll out a long, thin piece of clay that is thinner in the middle and thicker at the ends. Wrap it around the puppet's neck so that the thicker ends are left hanging. These are the arms. Let the puppet dry and harden.

Stick your puppet into a base made out of clay!

Seal

MATERIALS

air-drying clay—different colors
plastic knife
rolling pin
wire
scissors
1 toothpick

1 Roll out a long, thick piece of clay. Make a rounded point at one end for the head. Use a plastic knife to split the other end in two to make the back flippers.

2 Add eyes. Shape the seal's body.

3 For the front flippers, use a rolling pin to flatten out a piece of clay. Use the plastic knife to cut out a strip with pointed ends. Fold it over the back of the body.

4 Make a clay ball. Decorate it as you wish.

5 Stick little pieces of wire into the muzzle to make whiskers. Stick a toothpick into the nose and add the ball. Let the seal dry and harden.

The seal does tricks!

Starry Night

MATERIALS

air-drying clay–different colors
rolling pin
toothpick
plastic knife
wire

1 If you wish, you may mix two different colors of clay, such as orange and yellow, to make the stars. Use a rolling pin to flatten out the clay. Use a toothpick to draw two stars. Cut them out with the plastic knife.

2 You can mix blue and white clay for the cloud. Flatten it out with the rolling pin. Draw a cloud and cut it out.

3 For the moon, flatten out another piece of clay. Draw a half-moon and cut it out.

4 Draw a mouth with the toothpick. Add an eye and rosy cheek made out of clay.

5 Make a loop at one end of a piece of wire. Run the other end through the two stars, cloud, and moon. Let the mobile dry and harden.

Hang the mobile in your room!

Palm Tree

MATERIALS

air-drying clay—different colors
plastic knife
rolling pin
toothpick

1 Roll out a thick piece of clay for the trunk. One end should be a little thicker than the other.

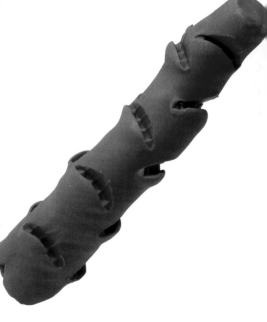

2 With the plastic knife, make notches along the tree trunk. Bend the trunk a little.

3 For the leaves, roll out four small, long pieces of clay. Flatten them out with the rolling pin.

10

4 Use the toothpick to make small lines in the leaves. Attach the leaves to the top of the trunk by pressing down with two fingers.

5 Make two balls out of clay for the coconuts. Add them to the tree. Let the tree dry and harden.

Now you have a coconut tree!

Round Box

MATERIALS

air-drying clay—different colors
rolling pin
plastic knife
white glue

1 Make a big ball of clay. Flatten the ball with the rolling pin. Cut out a circle with the plastic knife. This will be the base of the box.

2 Flatten another piece of clay. Add small pieces of a different colored clay to make stripes or any other decoration you want. Run the rolling pin over the stripes and big sheet of clay. Cut out a rectangle.

3 Wrap the rectangle around the base of the box. Cut off the extra clay.

4 Flatten another sheet of clay. Add polka dots or any other design you want. Cut out a circle that is the same size as the base. This will be the lid.

5 Make a cylinder out of clay. Cut a small piece. Glue it in the center of the lid. Let the box dry and harden.

Keep your things inside!

Snowman

1 Make two balls out of clay, one bigger than the other. Use the toothpick to stick them together.

MATERIALS

air-drying clay–different colors
1 toothpick
rolling pin
plastic knife
1 small wooden dowel

2 Add two eyes and a nose to the small ball of clay.

3 Using the rolling pin, make two sheets of clay. Add polka dots to one of the sheets and stripes to the another, if you wish. Run the rolling pin over them again.

4 For the hat, use the plastic knife to cut out half a circle from the striped sheet of clay. For the scarf, cut out a long, thin rectangle from the dotted sheet of clay. Attach the hat and scarf to the snowman.

5 For the broom, make a small clay triangle and cut a fringe into one of the sides. Stick the broom onto one end of the wooden dowel. Let the snowman dry and harden.

Brrrr!

Cactus

MATERIALS

small clay flowerpot
air-drying clay–different colors
toothpicks
scissors

1 Fill the flowerpot with clay. Stick a toothpick in the center.

2 Make four clay balls of different sizes. Flatten them a little with your hands.

3 Stick the biggest ball onto the toothpick in the flowerpot. Attach the other three smaller balls to the big ball with toothpicks.

4 Make the flowers with little balls of clay. Place them on the cactus.

5 Cut the pointy ends off several toothpicks. Stick them all around cactus. Let the cactus dry and harden.

Watch out for the spines!

Giraffe

MATERIALS

air-drying clay—different colors
5 small wooden dowels
rolling pin
plastic knife

1 Model the giraffe's body and tail out of clay.

2 Cover the five wooden dowels with clay. Stick four underneath the body to make the legs. Stick the fifth dowel into the top front end of the body to make the neck.

3 Model the giraffe's head from clay. Stick it on top of the neck.

18

4 Make the giraffe's patches and stick them onto the body. Put a tiny ball on each horn.

What a beautiful animal!

5 Use the rolling pin to flatten out a thin sheet of clay. Cut out five small rectangles with the plastic knife. Wrap four of them around the bottom of the legs to make the hooves. Cut a fringe into the fifth small rectangle. Wrap it around the end of the tail. Let the giraffe dry and harden.

Sandwich

air-drying clay–different colors
plastic knife
rolling pin
toothpick

1 Mold a piece of clay into a loaf of bread. Use the plastic knife to slice it in half. Carve lines into the top to make it look like crust.

2 To make the ham, run the rolling pin over a piece of clay. Cut out a rectangle.

3 Run the rolling pin over a piece of clay. Cut out some lettuce leaves. Use the toothpick to add lines.

4 For the cheese, run the rolling pin over a piece of clay. Cut out a rectangle and make holes.

5 Place the ham, cheese, and lettuce on the bottom half of the bread. Add the top half. Let the sandwich dry and harden.

It looks delicious!

Picture Frame

MATERIALS

cardboard
ruler
pencil
scissors
air-drying clay–different colo[r]
rolling pin
plastic knife
white glue

1 Cut out a rectangle from cardboard. Fold it in half. Use a ruler and pencil to draw a rectangle in the center of one of the halves. Cut it out. Glue the frame closed on three sides. Leave one side open so you can slip the picture inside.

2 Take three long pieces of clay and run the rolling pin over them a little.

3 Place the three strips of clay on top of each other. Run the rolling pin over them again. Cut off the ends with the plastic knife. Now you have a rectangle. Slice the rectangle into pieces.

22

4 Run the rolling pin over another piece of clay. Cut out four squares for the corners of the frame.

5 Spread glue along the frame's sides and add the colorful clay slices you made. Let everything dry.

Put your favorite picture inside.

Witch

1 Mold the witch's head out of clay. Add eyes, cheeks, and a mouth.

2 For the witch's body, run a rolling pin over a piece of clay to make a thick sheet. Roll out a long, thin piece of clay. Add polka dots or any other decoration you like to both pieces.

3 From the thick sheet of clay, cut out a rectangle (dress) and a half circle (hat) with the plastic knife.

4 Wrap the dress around the witch's neck. Wrap the long, thin piece of clay around the dress to create the arms.

5 For the hair, tie a bunch of raffia together. Press it into her head. Add the hat. Let the witch dry and harden.

She just needs a broom to fly!

Snail

MATERIALS

air-drying clay–different colors
rolling pin
plastic knife
toothpick

1 Roll out three different colored pieces of clay. Flatten them with the rolling pin.

2 Place the three pieces of clay on top of each other. Run the rolling pin over them again.

3 Roll up the clay strip and cut out a slice with the plastic knife. This circle will be the snail's shell.

4 Roll out a long, thick piece of clay for the snail's body. Shape it into an "S." Draw the mouth with the toothpick.

5 Add the eyes. Place the shell on the body. Let the snail dry and harden.

Slow down!

Boat

MATERIALS

air-drying clay–different colors
rolling pin
plastic knife
1 wooden dowel

1 Run the rolling pin over a piece of clay. Cut out a rectangle with the plastic knife.

2 Fold the rectangle in half and press the two short ends together.

3 Decorate the boat as you wish.

28

4 For the sail, use the rolling pin to flatten out another piece of clay. Decorate it as you wish.

5 Cut out a triangle and wrap it around the wooden dowel. Attach the sail to the boat.

Let's go sailing!

Portrait of a Bird

MATERIALS

air-drying clay–different colors
rolling pin
plastic knife
white glue
card stock

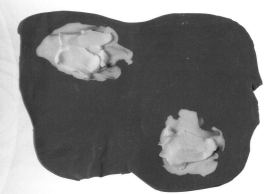

1 Use the rolling pin to flatten out a piece of blue clay. Add white clay for clouds.

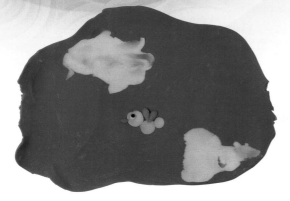

2 For the bird, place three small balls of clay (head and body) in the middle of the blue sky. Add the wings, beak, and eyes. Press them all in with your finger.

3 Run the rolling pin over the entire thing. Cut off the edges so you have a rectangle.

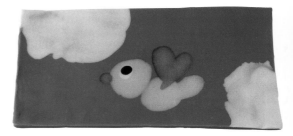

4 Flatten out another piece of clay. Cut out a rectangle a little larger than the blue one.

5 Glue the blue rectangle over the larger one. Glue this onto card stock. Let everything dry.

What a beautiful scene!

Read About

Books

The Bumper Book of Crafty Activities: 100+ Creative Ideas for Kids. Petaluma, Calif.: Search Press, 2012.

Hardy, Emma. *Green Crafts for Children.* New York: Ryland Peters & Small, 2008.

Kenney, Karen Latchana. *Super Simple Clay Crafts Projects: Fun and Easy-to-Make Crafts for Kids.* Minneapolis, Minn.: Abdo Publishing Company, 2009.

Internet Addresses

FamilyFun: Clay Crafts
<http://familyfun.go.com/crafts/crafts-by-material/clay-crafts/>

Family Education: Crafts for Kids
<http://fun.familyeducation.com/childrens-art-activities/crafts/32814.html>

Index
Easy to Hard